FRETBOARD BLUEGRASS
ROADMAPS AND FOLK

THE ESSENTIAL GUITAR PATTERNS THAT ALL THE PROS KNOW AND USE

T0041154

THE RECORDING
Guitar and Vocals—Fred Sokolow
Sound Engineer and Other Instruments—Dennis O'Hanlon
Recorded at O'Hanlon Recording and Music Services

PLAYBACK+
Speed • Pitch • Balance • Loop

To access audio visit:
www.halleonard.com/mylibrary

Enter Code
5925-4094-6096-7710

ISBN 978-0-634-00140-6

HAL•LEONARD®

Visit Hal Leonard Online at
www.halleonard.com

Contact us:
Hal Leonard
7777 West Bluemound Road
Milwaukee, WI 53213
Email: info@halleonard.com

In Europe, contact:
Hal Leonard Europe Limited
42 Wigmore Street
Marylebone, London, W1U 2RN
Email: info@halleonardeurope.com

In Australia, contact:
Hal Leonard Australia Pty. Ltd.
4 Lentara Court
Cheltenham, Victoria, 3192 Australia
Email: info@halleonard.com.au

CONTENTS

INTRODUCTION

Accomplished bluegrass and folk guitarists can *ad lib* hot solos and play backup in any key—all over the fretboard. They know several different soloing approaches and can choose the style that fits the tune, whether it's a blues-flavored country tune, hard driving bluegrass, or a pretty ballad with pop changes.

There are moveable patterns on the guitar fretboard that make it easy to do these things. The pros are aware of these "fretboard roadmaps," even if they don't read music. If you want to jam with other players, *this is essential guitar knowledge.*

You need the fretboard roadmaps if...

▶ All your soloing sounds the same and you want some different styles and flavors from which to choose.

▶ You don't know how to play in any key.

▶ Your guitar fretboard beyond the 5th fret is mysterious, uncharted territory.

▶ You can't automatically play any familiar melody .

▶ You know a lot of "bits and pieces" on the guitar, but you don't have a system that ties it all together.

Read on, and many mysteries will be explained. If you're serious about playing bluegrass and folk guitar, the pages that follow can shed light and save you a great deal of time.

Good luck,

Fred Sokolow

This book is a bluegrass and folk guitarist's extension of Fred Sokolow's *Fretboard Roadmaps* (Hal Leonard Corporation, HL00696514), which includes even more music theory for guitarists, along with musical examples, solos and licks. We urge you to use *Fretboard Roadmaps* as a reference, along with *Fretboard Roadmaps For Bluegrass & Folk Guitar*.

THE AUDIO AND PRACTICE TRACKS

All the licks, riffs and tunes in this book are played on the accompanying audio. There are also four *Practice Tracks*. Each has a standard bluegrass or folk groove and progression. They are mixed so that the lead guitar is on one side of your stereo and the backup band is on the other.

Each track illustrates the use of certain techniques, such as first position blues scales, or moveable chord-based licks.

You can also tune out the lead guitar track and use the backup tracks to practice playing solos.

NOTES ON THE FRETBOARD

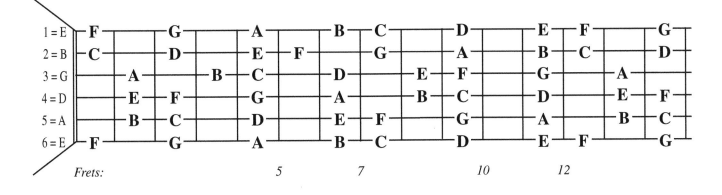

WHY?

▶ Knowing where the notes are (especially the notes on the 6th and 5th strings) will help you find chords and scales up and down the neck. It will help you alter and understand chords (e.g., *How do I flat the seventh in this chord? Why is this chord minor instead of major?*). It's a first step toward understanding music.

WHAT?

▶ *The notes get higher in pitch as you go up the alphabet and up the fretboard.*

▶ *A whole step is two frets, and a half step is one fret.*

▶ *Sharps are one fret higher:* 6th string/3rd fret = G, so 6th string/4th fret = G♯; 6th string/8th fret = C, so 6th string/9th fret = C♯.

▶ *Flats are one fret lower:* 6th string/5th fret = A, so 6th string/4th fret = A♭; 6th string/10th fret = D, so 6th string/9th fret = D♭.

HOW?

▶ *Fretboard markings help.* Most guitars have fretboard inlays or marks somewhere on the neck indicating the 5th, 7th, 10th and 12th frets. Become aware of these signposts.

DO IT!

▶ Start by memorizing the notes on the 6th and 5th strings. You will need to know these notes very soon—for **ROADMAP #4**.

SUMMING UP—NOW YOU KNOW...

▶ *The location of the notes on the fretboard*

▶ *The meaning of these musical terms:*

whole step, half step, sharp (♯), flat (♭)

THE MAJOR SCALE

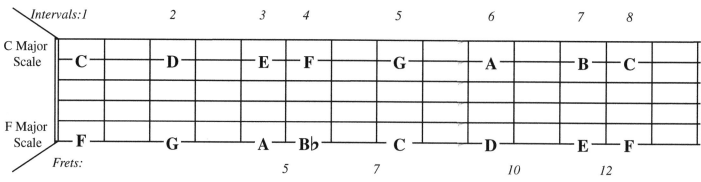

Intervals:	1		2		3	4		5		6		7	8
C Major Scale	C		D		E	F		G		A		B	C
F Major Scale	F		G		A	Bb		C		D		E	F
Frets:					5		7			10		12	

WHY?

▶ To understand music and to communicate with other players, you need to know about the major scale. The major scale is a ruler that helps you measure distances between notes and chords. Knowing the major scale will help you understand and talk about chord construction, scales and chord relationships.

WHAT?

▶ *The major scale is the "Do-Re-Mi" scale you have heard all your life.* Countless familiar tunes are composed of notes from this scale.

▶ *Intervals are distances between notes.* The intervals of the major scale are used to describe these distances. For example, E is the third note of the C major scale, and it is four frets above C (see above). This distance is called a *third*. Similarly, A is a third above F, and C♯ is a third above A. On the guitar, *a third is always a distance of four frets*.

HOW?

▶ *Every major scale has the same interval pattern of whole and half steps:*

	WHOLE		WHOLE	HALF	WHOLE		WHOLE		WHOLE	HALF	
C Major Scale	C		D		E	F		G		A		B	C
Intervals:	1		2		3	4		5		6		7	8

In other words, the major scale ascends and descends by whole steps (two frets at a time) with two exceptions: there is a half step (one fret) from the third to the fourth notes and from the seventh to the eighth notes. It's helpful to think of intervals in terms of frets (e.g., a third is 4 frets).

▶ *Intervals can extend above the octave.* They correspond to lower intervals:

C Major Scale

Intervals:

1	2	3	4	5	6	7	8	9	10	11	12	13
C	D	E F		G	A	B	C	D	E	F	G	A

Frets: 5   7   10   12   15   17   20

DO IT!

▶ *Learn the major scale intervals* by playing any note and finding the note that is a third higher, a fourth higher, etc.

SUMMING UP—NOW YOU KNOW...

▶ *The intervals of the major scale and the number of frets that make up each interval*

#3 FIRST POSITION MAJOR SCALES

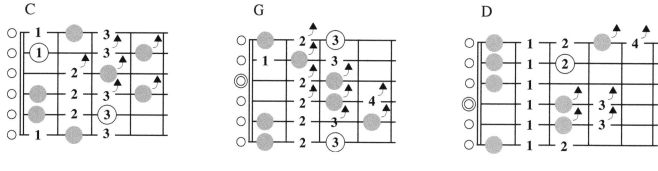

C   G   D

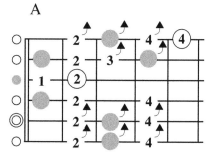   A   E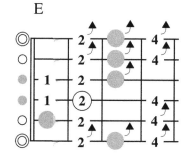

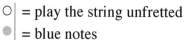

○ | = play the string unfretted

● | = blue notes

WHY?

▶ Whether they're playing a hot fiddle tune, picking the melody to a ballad or improvising a solo, bluegrass and folk guitarists use first position major scales often. Familiarity with these scales helps in all these areas.

WHAT?

▶ *Every key has its own scale and characteristic licks.* You use the C scale to play in the key of C, the E scale to play in E, and so on.

▶ *Each scale (and the licks that go with it) can be played throughout a tune,* in spite of chord changes within the tune.

▶ *A root is the note that gives the scale its name.*

▶ *The root notes in each scale are circled.* The numbers are suggested fingerings.

▶ *The grey circles are "blue notes,"* flatted 3rds, 5ths and 7ths. They add a bluesy flavor to the scales.

HOW?

▶ *Put your hand "in position" for each scale by fingering the appropriate chord* (e.g., play an E chord to get in position for the E major scale). You don't have to maintain the chord while playing the scale, but it's a reference point.

▶ *Play "up and down" each scale until it feels comfortable and familiar.* Play the chord before playing the scale, and "loop" the scale—play it several times in a row, with no pause between repetitions. Here are the five scales to practice:

2

C Major Scale

G Major Scale

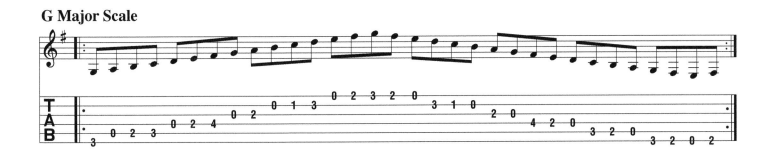

D Major Scale

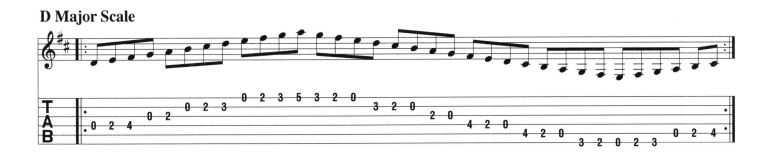

A Major Scale

E Major Scale

DO IT!

▶ The following solos show how to use all five major scales to play some classic licks. They are improvisations based on "Nine Pound Hammer," a bluegrass standard associated with Merle Travis.

❸ Nine Pound Hammer—C Major Scale

❹ Nine Pound Hammer—G Major Scale

❺ Nine Pound Hammer—D Major Scale

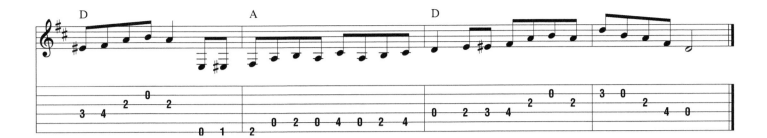

6

Nine Pound Hammer—A Major Scale

7

Nine Pound Hammer—E Major Scale

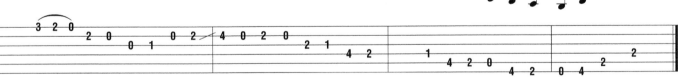

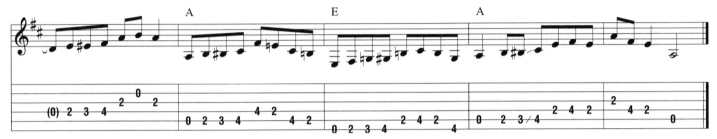

SUMMING UP — NOW YOU KNOW...

▶ *How to play five first-position major scales* (C, G, D, A and E) *and how to use them to play licks and solos*

▶ *The meaning of the musical term "blue notes," and how to add them to your major scales and licks*

#4 TWO MOVEABLE MAJOR CHORDS AND THEIR VARIATIONS

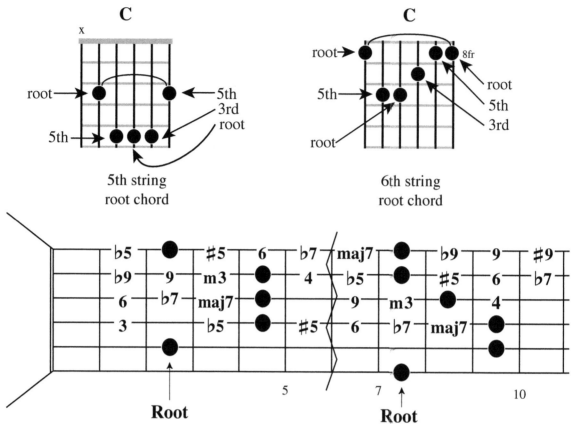

C — 5th string root chord

C — 6th string root chord

WHY?

▶ **ROADMAP #4** will help you build a full chord vocabulary. Some chords require the use of barred or moveable positions, and this chapter shows how to play nearly any chord you will need.

WHAT?

▶ A *chord* is a group of three or more notes played simultaneously.

▶ A *moveable chord* can be played all over the fretboard. It contains no open (unfretted) strings.

▶ A *root* is the note that gives a chord its name.

▶ *The two moveable major chords of* **ROADMAP #4** *(and all major chords) consist of roots, 3rds and 5ths.* Make sure you know the intervals in these two formations. The chord grids above **ROADMAP #4** identify the intervals (e.g., the 5th and 2nd strings in the barred E formation are 5ths).

▶ *You can play dozens of chords (minors, sevenths, major sevenths, etc.) by altering slightly the two basic, moveable major chords of* **ROADMAP #4.** For example, you can play one fret lower on one string to make a major chord minor. This is an easy way to expand your chord vocabulary.

HOW?

▶ *The 6th string identifies the 6th-string root/barred chord.* It's a G chord when played at the 3rd fret, because the 6th string/3rd fret is G. At the 6th fret it's a B♭ chord, and so on.

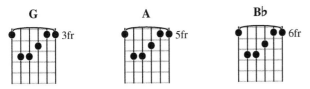

▶ *The 5th string identifies the 5th-string root/barred chord.* It's a C chord at the 3rd fret, because the 5th string/3rd fret is C. At the 9th fret it's F♯ (G♭), and so on.

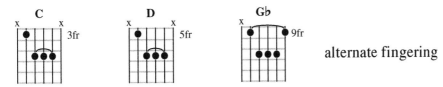

alternate fingering

▶ *There are four types of chords:*

▷ *Major chords* consist of a root (1), 3rd and 5th.

▷ *Minor chords* consist of a root, flatted 3rd and 5th.

▷ *Seventh chords* consist of a root, 3rd, 5th and flatted 7th.

▷ *Diminished chords* consist of a root, flatted 3rd, flatted 5th, and double-flatted 7th (which is the same as a 6th).

▶ *All other chords are variations of these four types.* For example:

▷ C6 is a C major chord with a 6th added (1, 3, 5, 6).

▷ Gm7♭5 (G minor seven, flat five) is a G minor chord with a flatted seventh and flatted 5th (1, ♭3, ♭5, ♭7).

▷ D7♭9+ (D seven flat nine, sharp five) is a D seventh chord with a flatted ninth and sharped (augmented) fifth (1, 3, ♯5, ♭7, ♭9). The + (augmented) notation almost always refers to the fifth.

DO IT!

▶ *Play the 6th-string root chords all over the fretboard,* naming the chords as you play them.

▶ *Play the 5th-string root chords all over the fretboard* and name them.

▶ *Compare every new chord you learn to a basic chord you already know.* Every small chord grid in the "DO IT" section below is a variation of a basic chord formation.

▶ *Here are the most-played chords.* Play them and compare each formation to the larger grid to the left, from which it is derived.

Major

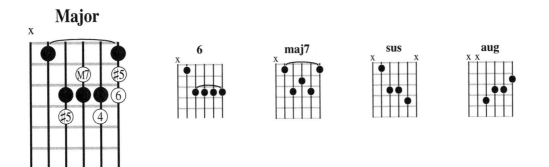

Minor

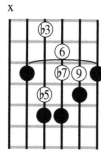

m7
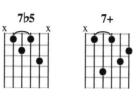

m6

m9

m7b5

Seventh

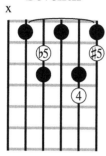

7b5
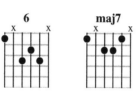

7+

7sus

Major

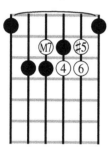

6

maj7

sus

aug

Minor

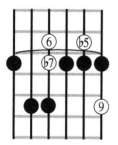

m7

m6

m9

m7b5

Seventh

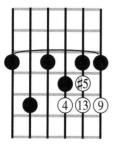

9
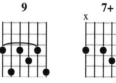

7+

7sus

13

Here is another very useful seventh shape with a 5th string root.

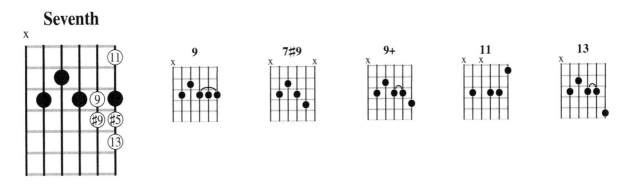

Diminished chords are seventh chords with a ♭3rd, ♭5th and ♭♭7th.

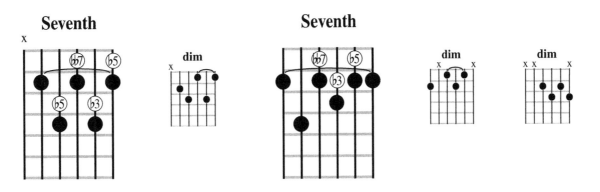

SUMMING UP—NOW YOU KNOW...

▶ *How to play any major chord two ways:* using a moveable chord with a 6th string root and a moveable chord with a 5th string root

▶ *The formulas for major, minor, 7th, and diminished chords,* and how to play them using moveable formations

▶ *How to vary the moveable major, minor, and 7th chords* to play many chord types: 9ths, 6ths, major sevenths, etc.

▶ *The meaning of these musical terms:*

chord, moveable chord, root

#5 **THE F-D-A ROADMAP**

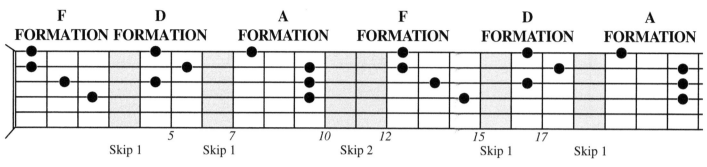

WHY?

▶ The **"F-D-A" ROADMAP** shows you how to play any major chord all over the fretboard, using three major chord formations. It's useful for improvising single-note and chord-style solos in all keys.

WHAT?

▶ The chords in the fretboard diagram above are all F chords.

HOW?

▶ *To memorize this roadmap,* remember: *F-SKIP 1, D-SKIP 1, A-SKIP 2.* In other words, play an F formation, skip a fret; play a D formation, skip a fret; play an A formation, skip two frets.

▶ Use the F-D-A roadmap to play all the D chords:

All D Chords:

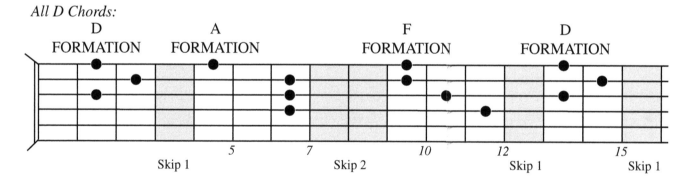

▶ Notice that you can climb the fretboard starting *with any chord formation.* The F–D–A roadmap is a continuous loop that you can enter at any point. It can be the D–A–F or A–F–D roadmap. The "skips" are always the same: one skip after F, one after D, two after A.

▶ You can add notes to the F, D, and A formations to create countless licks and *arpeggios.* (To play an arpeggio, pick each of the notes of a chord separately, going up or down in pitch.)

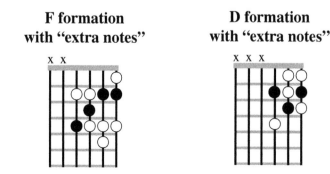
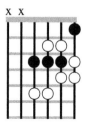

F formation with "extra notes"   **D formation with "extra notes"**   **A formation with "extra notes"**

8

G Arpeggio (F formation)   G Arpeggio (F formation with extra notes)

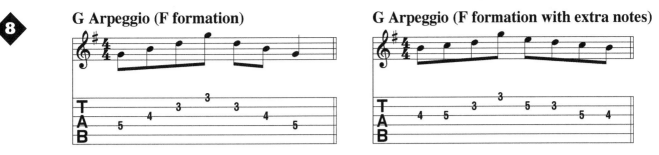

DO IT!

▶ *Play the following solo to the old folk song, "The Sloop John B."* It consists of ascending and descending chord fragments, enhanced by the "extra notes" pictured above.

9

The Sloop John B.

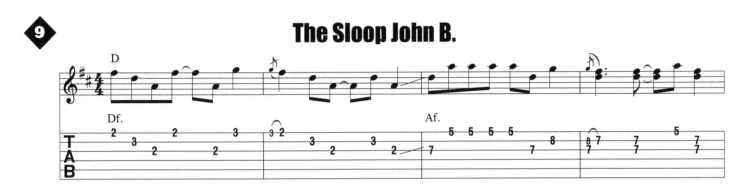

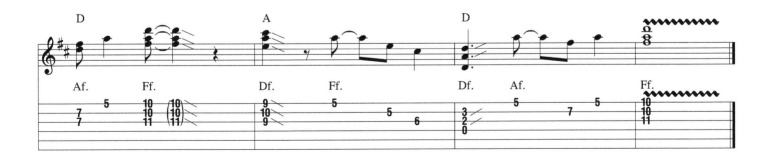

► *Use the F-D-A chords to play a solo to the country standard, "Wabash Cannonball,"* using arpeggios to create a fingerpicking sound.

Wabash Cannonball—With Arpeggios

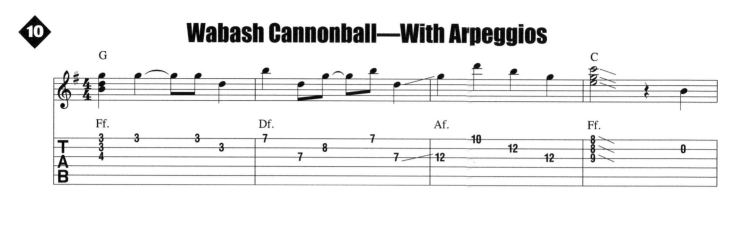

► Here's another solo based on the F-D-A chords. "The Great Speckled Bird," popularized by Roy Acuff, has the same melody as "I'm Thinking Tonight of my Blue Eyes," "The Prisoner's Song," "Wild Side of Life," and many other country/bluegrass standards.

The Great Speckled Bird

SUMMING UP — NOW YOU KNOW...

▶ *How to play three major chord fragments*

▶ *How to use them to play any major chord all over the fretboard* (with the F–D–A roadmap)

▶ *How to alter them to create countless licks and arpeggios*

▶ *How to play moveable licks and solos, based on chord fragments*

▶ *The meaning of the musical term "arpeggio"*

Three B♭ Chord Families

● = I
○ = IV
◉ = V

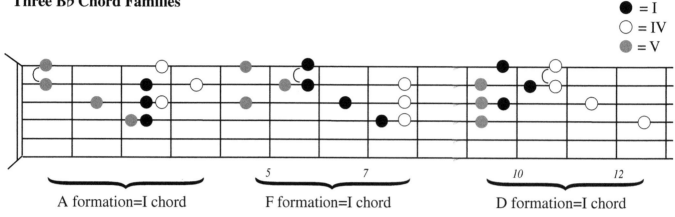

A formation=I chord   F formation=I chord   D formation=I chord

WHY?

▶ It's easier to learn new tunes and create solos when you understand "chord families" and know how to play them all over the fretboard. **ROADMAP #6** arranges the three chord fragments of **ROADMAP #5** into chord families.

WHAT?

▶ *Every song has a chord progression,* a repeated chord sequence in which each chord is played for a certain number of bars.

▶ *Thousands of tunes consist of just three chords: the I, IV and V chord. These three chords are a "chord family."* "I," "IV," and "V" refer to the major scale of your key.

▷ The I chord is the key. In the key of C, C is the I chord, because C is the first note in the C major scale.

▷ The IV chord is the chord whose root is the fourth note in the major scale of your key. In the key of C, F is the IV chord, since F is the fourth note in the C major scale.

▷ The V chord is the chord whose root is the fifth note in the major scale of your key. In the key of C, G is the V chord, since G is the fifth note in the C scale.

▶ **ROADMAP #6** *shows three ways of playing the "key of G" chord family:* with an F formation/I chord, a D formation/I chord, and an A formation/I chord.

▶ *The relationships in* **ROADMAP #6** *are moveable. Once you learn them, you can make chord changes automatically.* For example, in any key, if you're playing a I chord with an F formation, the V chord is the D formation one fret lower.

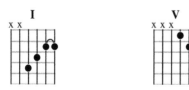

DO IT!

▶ *This solo to a standard I–IV–V progression will give you some practice memorizing the chord family relationships.*

▶ In this I–V–IV–I progression, the solo consists of chord fragment arpeggios. Using **ROADMAP #6**, you could easily play the same solo in any key.

► Countless bluegrass standards have a I–IV–I–V progression similar to the following blue-grass standard, "Wreck of Old 97." The ad-lib guitar solo makes use of two moveable, key-of-G chord families. The chord-licks include slides, *hammer-ons and pull-offs*.

▷ To play a hammer-on, sound a note by fretting a string suddenly with your fretting finger (rather than picking it with your picking hand).

▷ To play a pull-off, sound a note by plucking downward on a string.

Wreck of Old 97

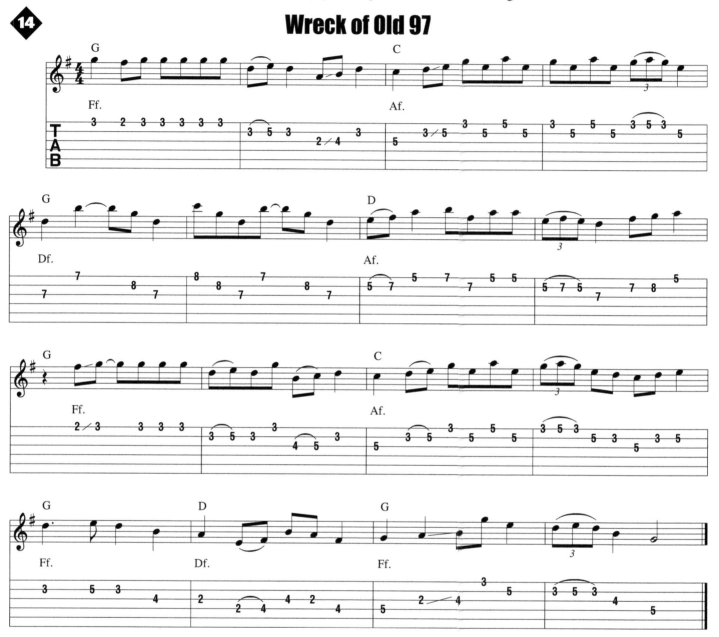

► *Many bluegrass, country and folk standards are based on the 12-bar blues progression.* "T for Texas," "I'm Movin' On," "Move It on Over," "Folsom Prison Blues," "Honky Tonk Blues" and "Muleskinner Blues" are a few examples. Here's a 12-bar blues in A:

Key of A

Each of the 12 bars (measures) in the above blues progression has 4 beats.

The repeat sign ✗ means play another bar of the chord in the previous bar.

► *The following chord-based solo features many "blue notes"* (flatted thirds, fifths and sevenths). Before you play it, here's how to add blue notes to the three chord fragments (the F, D and A formations):

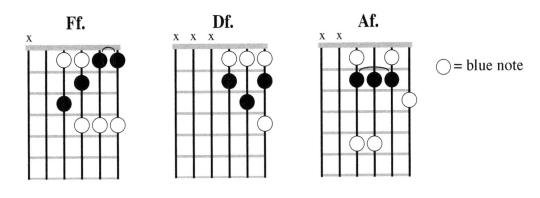

○ = blue note

Blue Note Boogie

SUMMING UP—NOW YOU KNOW...

► *How to locate three different chord families for any key, using chord fragments*

► *How to use all three chord fragment/chord families to play licks, arpeggios and solos*

► *How to add "blue notes" to the chord fragments*

► *The meaning of these musical terms:*

   I Chord, IV Chord, V Chord, Chord Family, 12-Bar Blues, Blue Notes, Hammer-on, Pull-off

#7 MOVEABLE MAJOR SCALES

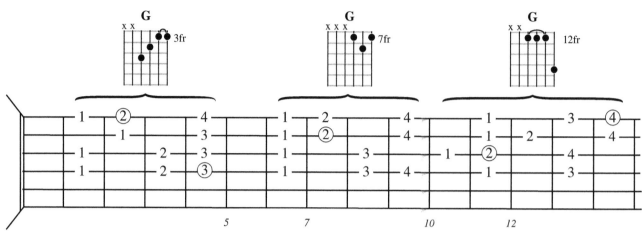

WHY?

▶ The moveable major scales help you play melodies and ad lib solos in any key, all over the fretboard. They bring you a step closer to any player's goal: to be able to *play* whatever you can hear.

WHAT?

▶ *The numbers on the fretboard in* ROADMAP #7 *are left-hand fingering suggestions.*

▶ *The three scales of* ROADMAP #7 *are based on the three chord fragments* of ROADMAPS #5 and #6. The root notes (all G's in this diagram) are circled. Play the appropriate chord fragment to get your fretting hand "in position" to play one of the major scales. For example, play an F formation at the 3rd fret to play the lowest G scale of ROADMAP #7.

HOW?

▶ *Here are the three G scales that match the three G chord fragments.* Play the chord fragment before playing the scale. Start each scale with its root note so you can recognize the "do-re-mi" sound you have heard all your life! Then play the major scale exercise that follows; it's a great warm-up.

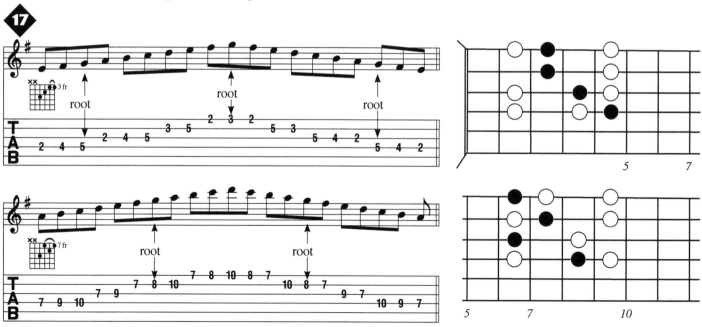

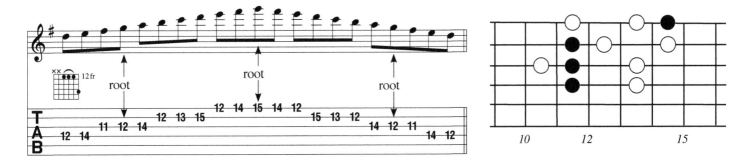

▶ *You can base a solo on the major scale that matches a song's key.* If a song is in the key of C, you can often ad lib C major scale licks throughout, even though the song has many chord changes.

DO IT!

▶ *Use major scales to play fiddle tunes.* Here are a few favorites:

Arkansas Traveler

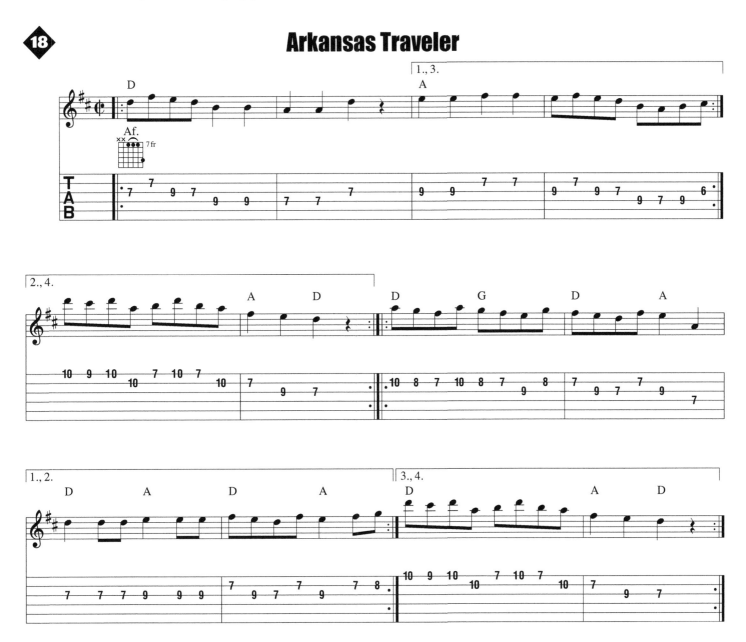

Turkey in the Straw

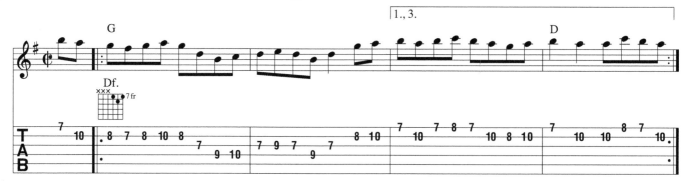

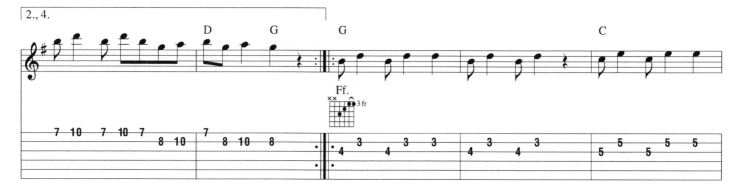

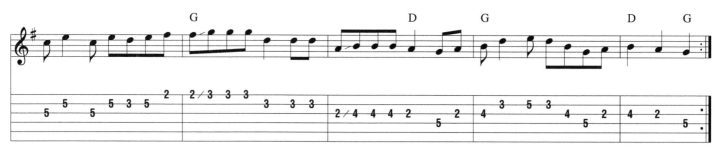

Soldiers' Joy

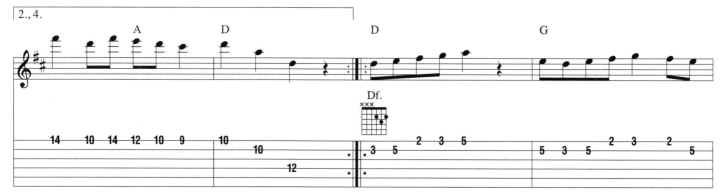

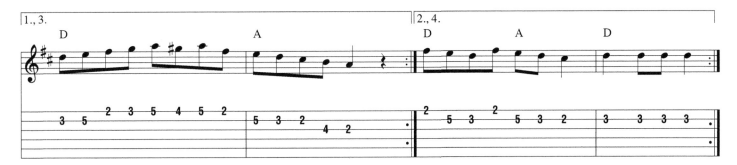

▶ *Use major scales to jam.* Make up short three or four note phrases by going up and down the major scale of a song's key. As long as you stay in the scale, none of the notes will be *wrong,* and through practice and trial-and-error, you'll learn to improvise. The following solo to the old country tune "Redwing" shows how it's done. The solo makes use of three G major scales:

Redwing

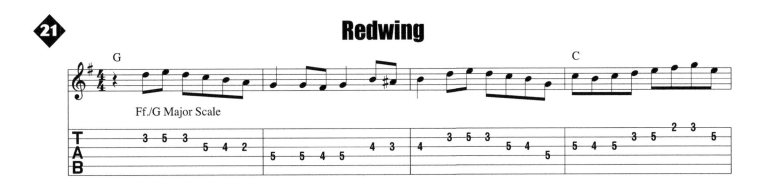

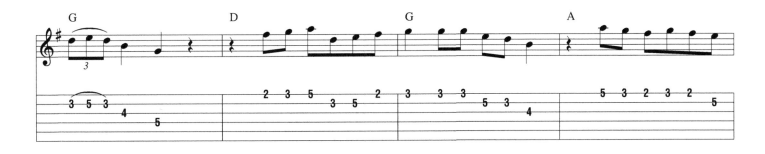

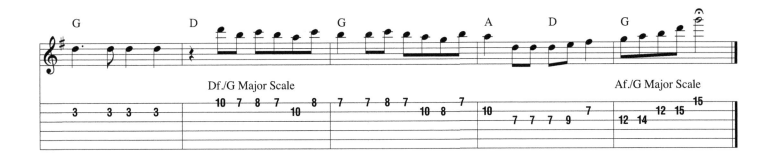

► *Use major scales to play melodic solos.* "Bury Me Beneath the Willow," below, shows how to embellish a melody with slides, fiddle-tune-like scales and ad lib licks.

Bury Me Beneath the Willow

► *If a song stays on a chord for a long time (4 or more bars), base your soloing on the major scale for that chord.* In "Banks of the Ohio" below, the soloist plays A major scales but switches to E scales for the 4 bars of E chord near the beginning of the song.

Banks of the Ohio

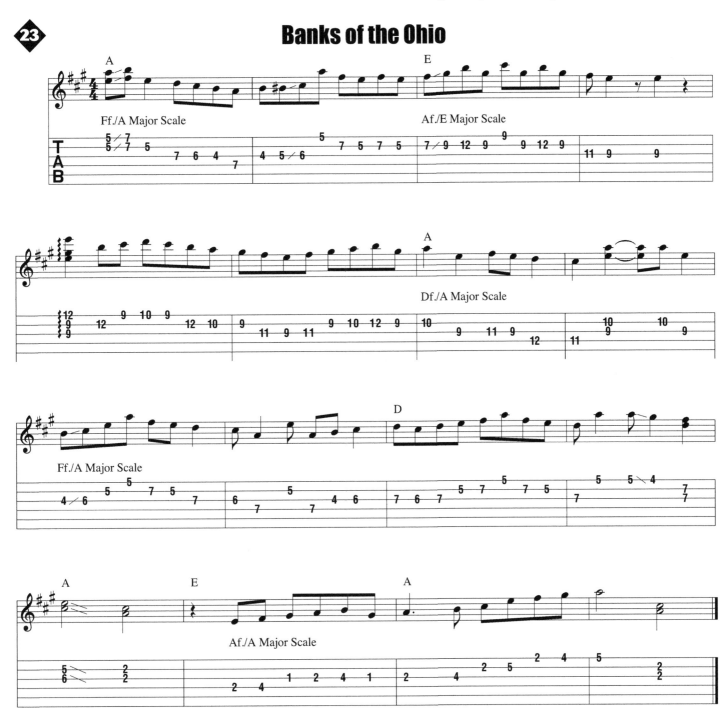

SUMMING UP—NOW YOU KNOW...

► *How to play three moveable major scales for each key*

► *How to use them to play fiddle tunes*

► *How to use them to ornament a melody and ad lib solos*

MAJOR SCALE "DOUBLE-NOTE" LICKS

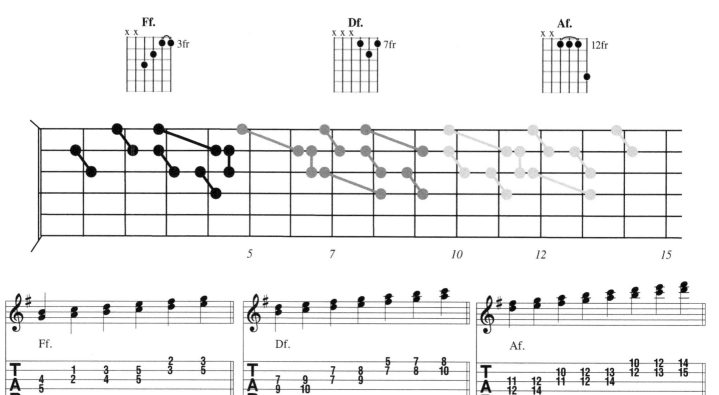

WHY?

► These moveable double-note patterns are embellishments of the major scales of **ROADMAP #7**. Often used in bluegrass music, they can also lend a South-of-the-border ("Tex-Mex"), Caribbean or Hawaiian flavor.

WHAT?

► *These double-note patterns are G major scales, harmonized with thirds.*

► *The three patterns are based on the major scales of the previous chapter, which in turn are based on the F, D and A formations of* **ROADMAPS #5** *and* **#6**.

HOW?

► *Like major scales, each pattern can be used throughout a song.* In the key of G, you can ad lib solos using any of the three patterns shown above.

DO IT!

► *Use the double-note licks as fills and in solos.* The following bluegrass version of "Nine Pound Hammer" features double-note fills during the vocal portion and a solo that mixes double-note licks with single-note, chord-based licks.

Nine Pound Hammer

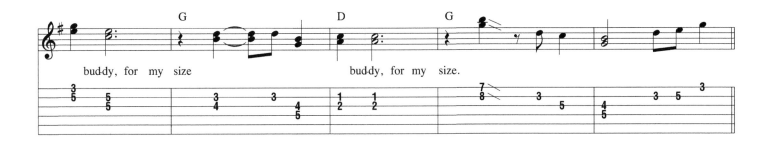

The nine pound ham-mer is a lit-tle too heav-y,

bud-dy, for my size   bud-dy, for my size.

► *Here's a solo to "Careless Love" that features double-note licks:*

Careless Love

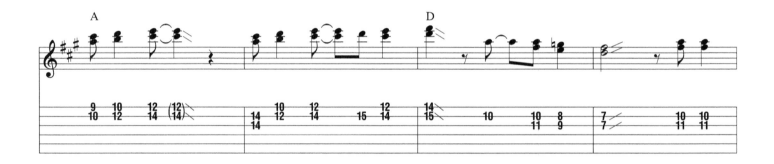

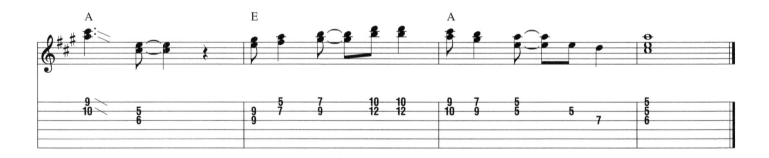

SUMMING UP—NOW YOU KNOW...

► *How to harmonize three moveable major scales with thirds*

► *How to use the harmonized scales for licks and solos*

 **TWO MOVEABLE BLUES BOXES**

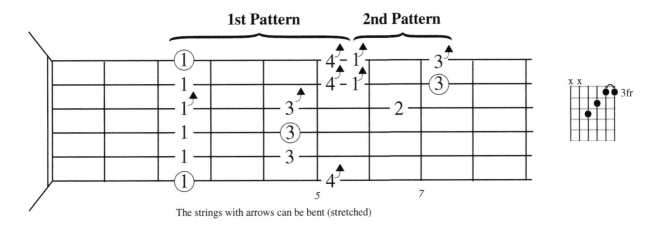

1st Pattern **2nd Pattern**

The strings with arrows can be bent (stretched)

WHY?

▶ The moveable scales of this **ROADMAP**, often called *blues boxes*, are the basis for modern blues and rock guitar, and they are often used in country, folk and bluegrass music.

WHAT?

▶ *The two blues boxes above are G blues scales.* The root notes are circled. The numbers indicate suggested fingering positions.

▶ *Often, you can solo in one blues box throughout a song, in spite of chord changes.*

▶ *The scale notes with arrows* 3↗, 4↗ *can be stretched or choked, or you can slide up a fret from these notes, to create a bluesy effect.* Stretching a string (pulling a string up or down with your fretting finger to raise its pitch) is an important blues sound.

stretching a string

▶ *The blues boxes are pentatonic,* which means they contain five notes. However, you can add other notes and still sound bluesy.

F Blues Scale with "Extra Notes"

1st Pattern   2nd Pattern

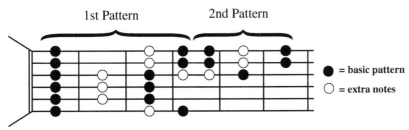

● = basic pattern
○ = extra notes

HOW?

► *To put your left hand in position for the first blues box, play an F formation at the appropriate fret.* For the key of G, play an F formation at the third fret, which is a G chord. Here's the scale:

First Blues Box, Key of G

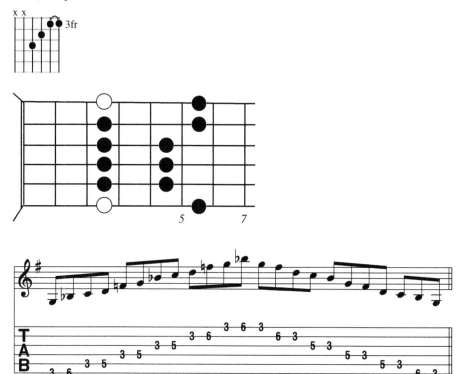

► *To put your left hand in position for the second blues box, play the root note on the second string with your third (ring) finger.* In G, play the G note on the 2nd string/8th fret with your ring finger. Here's the scale:

Second Box, Key of G

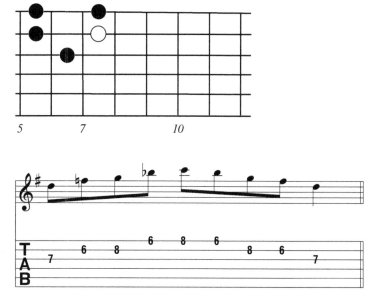

DO IT!

▶ *Use the blues boxes to ad lib solos.* The following solo illustrates the use of both key-of-G blues boxes in the bluegrass standard "Roll in My Sweet Baby's Arms."

Roll in My Sweet Baby's Arms

► *Use the blues boxes to play in minor keys.* The following solo to the classic gospel tune, "Wayfaring Stranger" in Am, is based on A blues boxes.

Wayfaring Stranger

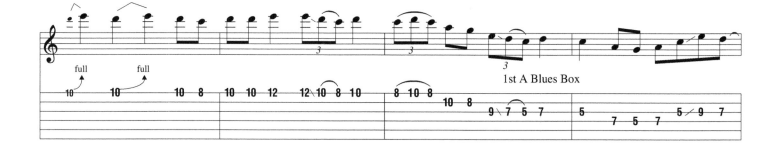

► ***Relative minor blues scale substitution:*** When a song doesn't call for a bluesy feel, you can still use the first and second blues boxes—just play them *three frets lower than the song's actual key.*

For example, the following version of the old gospel song "Mary, Don't You Weep" is in the key of C. Instead of using the first C blues box, at the 8th fret, start three frets lower, at the 5th fret, and use the first and second A blues boxes.

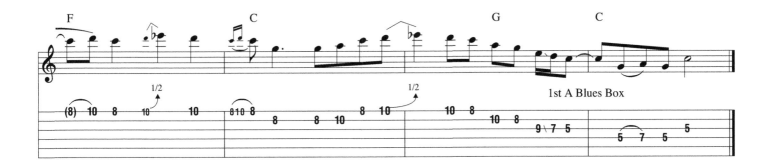

SUMMING UP—NOW YOU KNOW...

► *Two moveable blues boxes*

► *Many licks that go with each box*

► *How to use the boxes to improvise single-note solos in any key, major or minor*

► *How to substitute the relative minor blues scale when blues boxes don't fit in a tune*

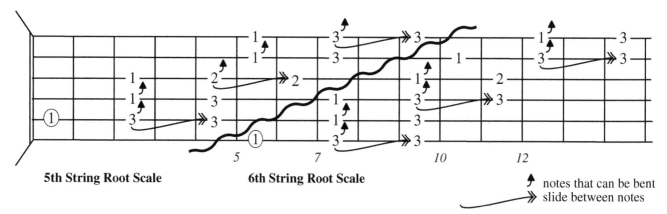

5th String Root Scale   6th String Root Scale

↑ notes that can be bent
≫ slide between notes

WHY?

▶ These two versatile scales are important to any lead guitarist. They're useful in country, rock, folk and bluegrass, and in simple three-chord tunes, and songs with many chord changes.

WHAT?

▶ There are two B♭ scales in **ROADMAP #10**. *One has a 6th string root, the other a 5th string root.* Both roots are circled.

▶ *These scales include "built-in" slides,* indicated by long arrows. As a result, each "sliding scale" spans ten frets.

▶ *Numbers on the fretboard with short arrows (3↑, 1↑) can be stretched* (choked).

▶ *Often, one sliding scale can be played throughout a tune.* If a tune is in the key of C, you can use C sliding scales throughout.

▶ *You can also "go with the changes"* and use the sliding scale that matches each chord change, especially when a song stays on a chord for more than a few bars.

▶ *The major pentatonic scale contains these five notes: 1, 2, 3, 5 and 6.* In the key of C, that's: C(1), D(2), E(3), G(5), A(6).

HOW?

▶ *Play both sliding scales over and over to become familiar with them.*

31

C Sliding Scale—5th String Root

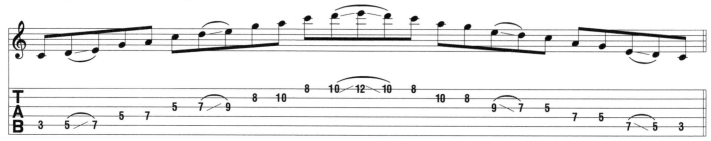

C Sliding Scale—6th String Root

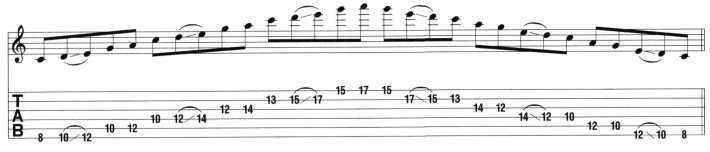

DO IT!

▶ *Play the following solo to "Wreck of Old 97."* It consists of B♭ sliding scale licks.

32

Wreck of Old 97

5th String Root/B♭ Sliding Scale

6th String Root/
B♭ Sliding Scale

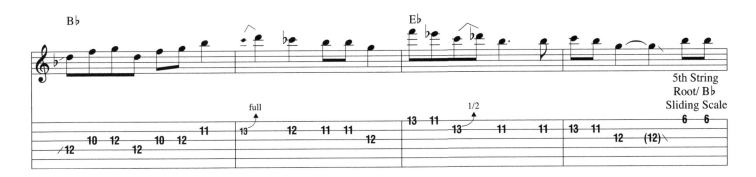

5th String
Root/ B♭
Sliding Scale

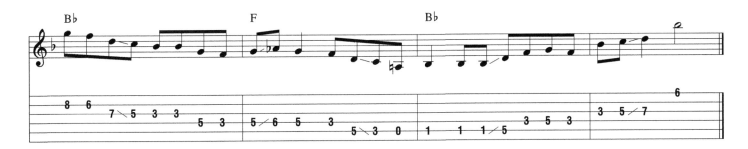

► *The following solo to "Worried Man Blues" goes "with the changes."* It's in the key of G and includes G, C and D sliding scales.

Worried Man Blues

6th String Root/G Sliding Scale

5th String Root/C Sliding Scale

6th String Root/G Sliding Scale

5th String Root/D Sliding Scale

6th String Root/G Sliding Scale

► *Here's a sliding scale-based solo to "Take This Hammer."*

Take This Hammer

5th String Root/C Sliding Scale

6th String Root/G Sliding Scale

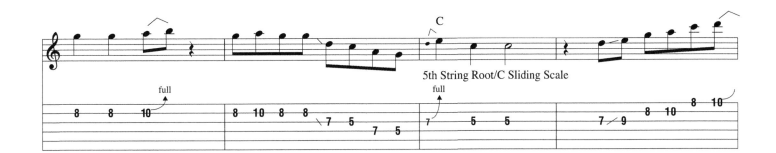

5th String Root/C Sliding Scale

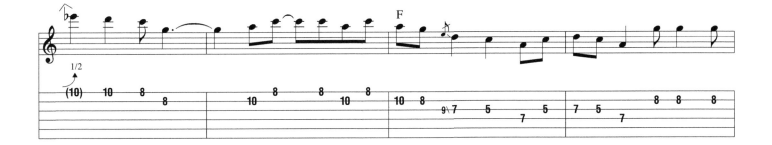

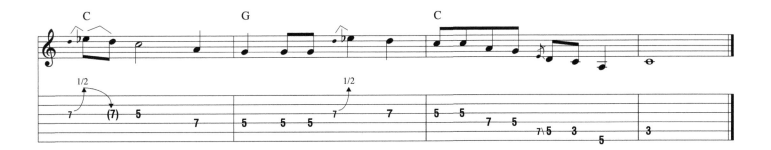

SUMMING UP—NOW YOU KNOW....

► *Two sliding pentatonic scales for each key and how to use them for soloing*

ANOTHER MOVEABLE "DOUBLE-NOTE" LICK

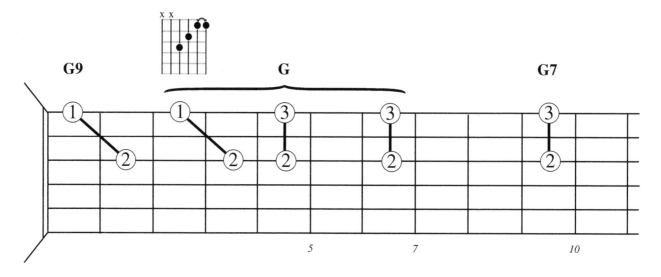

WHY?

▶ This moveable double-note pattern is the basis for many licks and tag endings, including the famous "blue yodel" lick.

WHAT?

▶ *"Home base" for this series of licks is the F formation.* To play G licks, position your fretting hand at the third fret/F formation.

▶ *There are countless double-note licks* that spring from this roadmap. They can go up, down, or up and down, as shown by these variations on a G chord:

"Blue Yodel" lick

▶ *The ninth and seventh chords (shown in ROADMAP #11) offer still more variations.* See examples in the "DO IT" section.

HOW?

▶ *Change F formations with the tune's chord changes:* when there is a C chord, play double-note licks based on the F formation/C chord at the 8th fret.

▶ *You can start a lick at any of the five positions of* **ROADMAP #11**—not just at the F formation.

DO IT!

▶ *Use the double-note licks as fills and in solos.* The following solo to "Amazing Grace" features double-note licks mixed with the chord-based soloing of **ROADMAPS #5** and **#6**.

Amazing Grace

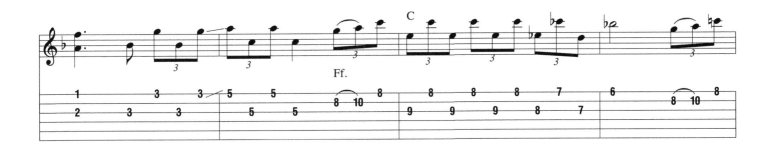

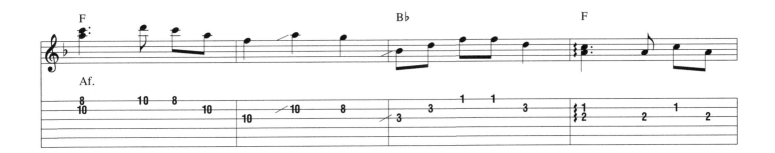

► *"Corinne Corinna" below, mostly consists of double-note licks. Notice how the 7th and 9th positions (labeled in the music/tab) lead up a IVth: C9 leads to F, and G7 leads to C.*

Corinne Corinna

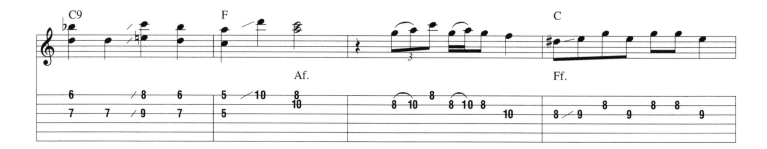

SUMMING UP—NOW YOU KNOW...

► *How to play a series of double-note licks on the 1st and 3rd strings for solos or backup, in any key*

► *How to play the "blue yodel" lick*

► *That 7th or 9th chords often lead "up a fourth"*

#12 USING THE CAPO

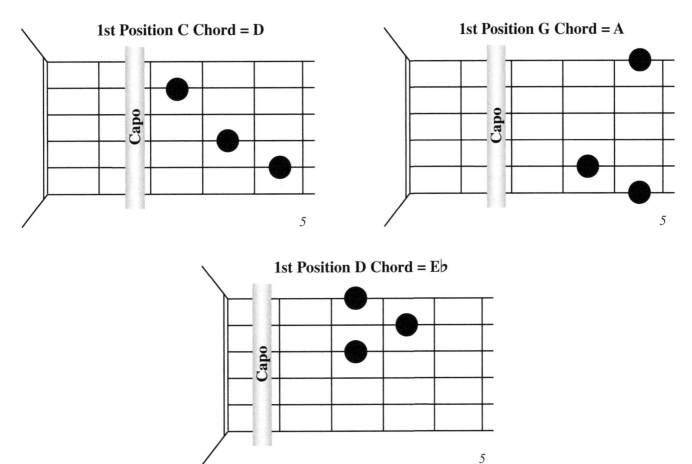

1st Position C Chord = D

1st Position G Chord = A

1st Position D Chord = E♭

WHY?

▶ Folk and bluegrass guitarists tend to play in first position, in the keys that include open strings (C, G, D, A and E), because the sound of open strings ringing out is an intrinsic part of the music. The capo makes it possible to play this way in all keys.

▶ You can also use the capo to raise the pitch of an *arrangement*. For example: many traditional fiddle tunes are played in D and A (easy keys for violin). On guitar, these tunes are easier to play in C and G. The capo can raise your C arrangements to the key of D, and your G arrangements to the key of A, so you can play with a fiddler.

WHAT?

▶ Some guitarists have a snobbish attitude about the capo, but the long list of legendary pickers who used a capo includes Muddy Waters, Doc Watson, Chet Atkins, Bo Diddley, Keith Richards, Ry Cooder, Robert Johnson, Lester Flatt and Andres Segovia.

▶ *Clamping a capo around the guitar neck raises the instrument's pitch.* If you capo at the first fret and play a first position G chord, it sounds like G♯. With the capo at the second fret, a first position G sounds like A.

▶ *Moveable chords are not affected by the capo.* If the capo is on the first fret, a barred G chord at the actual 3rd fret is still a G chord. But a barred G chord three frets above the capo is G♯.

HOW?

▶ *To play in a difficult key like Eb or B, go backwards in the alphabet a step or two, and capo as many steps up the neck.*

▷ To play in Eb, go a half-step (one fret) back in the alphabet, to D. Capo at the first fret and play a D chord.

▷ All the other chords in the Eb arrangement will go "back a half-step." For Ab, play a G chord. For Bb7, play A7, and so on.

▷ You could also go one and a half steps (three frets) back in the alphabet, to C, and capo at the third fret. Eb chords are now C chords, Ab is F, and so on.

▶ *To move a guitar arrangement to a higher key, go forward in the alphabet and capo as many steps up the neck.*

▷ To move (transpose) your key-of-G arrangement of a fiddle tune to the key of A, capo on the second fret, because A is a whole step (two frets) above G.

▷ If you've learned a key-of-C arrangement of a song but your voice would be more comfortable in the key of E, capo at the 4th fret. E is two whole steps (four frets) above C.

▶ The following chart shows how to use the capo to play in any key. It offers choices for most keys.

To Play in the Key of	Capo at Fret #	and Play a 1st Position
Ab	1	G
	4	E
A	2	G
	5	E
Bb	1	A
	3	G
B	2	A
	4	G
C	3	A
	5	G
Db	1	C
	4	A
D	2	C
Eb	1	D
	3	C
E	2	D
	4	C
F	1	E
	3	D
	5	C
Gb	2	E
	4	D
	6	C
G	3	E
	7	C

DO IT!

▶ *Make sure you can use the capo to solve these problems:*

▷ You've learned to play the fiddle tune "Sally Goodin" in G, but your fiddler friend plays it in A. Where do you put the capo to play with him? (As the preceding capo chart shows, you can capo on the 2nd fret and play your G arrangement.)

▷ A songbook has one of your favorite tunes written in the key of E♭. You can sing it in that key, but how can you use the capo to make it easier to play? (Consulting the capo chart again, capo on the 3rd fret and play in the key of C. Where the book says "E♭," play a C. Similarly, all chords will be three frets lower than the ones in the book: for A♭, play F; for B♭7, play G7, and so on.)

▷ You want to learn a song from an album. The artist sings it in the key of B♭, which is too low for your voice. What do you do? (You could play it in C, which is two frets higher than B♭, or D, which is 4 frets higher. No capo is needed, either way.)

▷ Another song on the same album is in F, and it's too high for your voice. What do you do? (D is three frets lower than F, and C is five frets lower. If D is right for your voice, you could play in D without a capo, or play in C with the capo on the second fret.)

SUMMING UP—NOW YOU KNOW...

▶ *How to use a capo to play in any key using first position chords*

▶ *How to use a capo to raise the key of a guitar arrangement*

▶ *How to use a capo to change a song's key to suit your voice*

USING THE PRACTICE TRACKS

The **ROADMAPS** illuminate many soloing styles, including:

▶ *First Position Major Scales*

▶ *Chord Fragment Licks*

▶ *Blues Boxes*

▶ *Substitute Blues Boxes*

▶ *Sliding Pentatonic Scales*

▶ *Moveable Major Scales*

▶ *Moveable Double-Note Major Scales*

▶ *Another Moveable Double-Note Set Of Licks*

On the four practice tracks, the lead guitar is separated from the rest of the band—it's on one side of your stereo. You can tune it out and use the band as backup, trying out any soloing techniques you like. You can also imitate the lead guitar. Here are the soloing ideas on each track:

 #1 **"Bury Me Beneath The Willow"** (in G) — During this I–IV–I–V tune, the soloist uses the first position G major scale to play the melody, and switches to chord fragment licks the second and third times around the progression.

 #2 **"Take This Hammer"** (in E) — The first time around, the soloist plays first position/E major scale licks with plenty of blue notes and blues licks thrown in. The second chorus consists mostly of E and B sliding scale licks; the third solo is based on chord fragments, including first and third string/double note licks.

 #3 **"Wabash Cannonball"** (in C) — The first solo is based on first position C major scales. The second and third time around the 16-bar tune, the solo consists of moveable major scales. The third solo features the double-note major scale licks of Roadmap #8 .

 #4 **"Chilly Winds"** (in D) — In this old folk tune, which is sometimes called "Lonesome Road Blues," the first solo uses the first position D major scale to express the melody. The second solo is based on "substitute" (key-of-B) moveable blues scales, and the third on moveable D blues scales.